A Brief Story of an Exceptional Divorce: A Recollective Tale from the Kid's Eyes

By
Alec Thein

A Brief Table of Contents

<u>Forewarning</u>

Before we get into the thick of this occurrence, happening, or whatever synonym you can think of, that seems to affect so many relationships today, I need to get something off my chest. This book has no other intention, other than to hopefully assist or enlighten whoever reads it with the fact, and I really emphasize the word "fact," that whether it is you, the parent, or you, the child, you must throw away or at least set aside all of the former ideas you initially had about divorce. Go into this as if it was a brand new, undiscovered place, ready to explore, albeit a crazy one. I have, and always will love both of my parents equally, despite all of the things, minor or major, that happened.

So I preface with this, only because, from someone who has had divorced parents for almost fifteen years now, it does in fact get better, not that it was ever "bad." This book is not a memoir of my entire life, or a tutorial on how to cope with divorce, but merely an aid or a look into a different perspective to help one understand what it is like for a kid who, and dare I say it, survived my parents' divorce. Think of what you are about to read as a peek into my life, if you will. Now, I'm most certainly not an expert on this matter at all, nor am I a psychologist, as I am sure you will realize as you read. Although, I would consider myself more than familiar with the subject. So don't expect extensive research, or hard facts about the study of the topic, because this is simply the experience I had with my parents' divorce, and the aftermath of it.

For Mom and Dad: Even though you two know how I felt, and feel about your divorce, I hope this book expresses my true feelings towards it, not that they're any different than what you know. I think we all turned out better than ever, and we all certainly know it. This is me, attempting to at least partially return the favor by sharing your story, for the absolute infinite number of things you've both done for me. Every day, I become more and more proud that I get to be your son. I love you both, more than life.

A special thanks to Cynthia. This book wouldn't have come together without you.

The story you are about to read consists of the author's current memories of experiences that occurred throughout the book. Names have been changed, descriptions and particular attributes have been altered, and events have been compressed.

Divorce I

Divorce is weird, upsetting, ignorant, healthy, whatever you want to call it. We all know marriages usually begin in the utmost fashion. Long-time best friends finally taking a chance formally molding a concrete, romantic relationship, or a random meeting from two polar opposite strangers that blossoms into a stunning bind of love. Okay, you know how marriages can start, and I think we can go all day long on how people meet, but this isn't about how marriages start; it's about how they end, and the effects that the ending has on the family. So to all of the children of divorce out there, if it is in fact you that happens to be reading this, let me flat out tell you, if your parents are going through a divorce or are in the process of it, this is important: _It is not just about you_. I want to make that extremely clear right off the bat here because it is crucial purely for your mental health in the scheme of things. Even if you think the divorce is because of you (it isn't), take yourself out of the equation. There will always be underlying reasons, or factors that are obvious, but it's absolutely imperative for the kids to realize that they should stay out of the supposed crossfire of the divorce. Getting in between things will only exacerbate everything that is going on. I do want to make a brief distinction, though, between the two perspectives of the parents and children. Parents, please do not put your children in a shoddy position, where they will be forced to make choices they should not have to make, because of you. Plotting against your significant other just to make them look inferior to you as a parent won't do anything but make the circumstances worse. The entire situation should be smooth for the kids, considering they are already going through the event of their parents splitting up.

With all of that being said, I believe there are three loose stages of divorce, and it's pretty simple. There is the before, which is the build up, every little thing that causes or seems to further taint the relationship between two people. That leads up to the second stage, or as I'll refer to it, 'the course'. The course is the process in which the divorce is actually happening. Papers are starting to get filed, new homes are being considered, living arrangements for the children are discussed, and final, wishful marriage-saving questions are asked. This is the stage where the knife is inserted and dragged through the once-sweet, now-rotten fruit that is the parents' marriage. The course is also the part where one of, if not, both of the parents attempt to salvage the relationship before it really does end. Sometimes it works, but other times, including my parents' situation, it does not work. And with that, finally, there's the after, which is usually the most diverse, and vastly different of the stages. It's everything after the official split. In this period, although it's certainly possible, rarely does the same ending happen for each family. Some are completely broken, some are mended back together, and others are stitched back with the help of some long, nostalgic talks about the good times, where that tethered love doesn't seem to escape one's mind.

Listen, I don't intend for theses stages to become the new thing shown at seminars and discussed in therapy rooms. These stages can be skipped, or avoided completely, and will most likely be different for everyone. Those three stages can assist one in breaking down each part of the divorce, and possibly help bring some light as to why this whole mess happened. One doesn't simply get married, then proceed to immediately have a child, then get divorced without reason.

Now begins the story of my experience with divorce. Before I start this tale of a few twists, but mostly turns, I want to make one thing clear: this story is told completely through my eyes from the age of a child to an adult, not as a parent, purely from memory. Everything I speak about is what I saw, remember, and went through. This story is told strictly through my perspective, and mine only, as well the things that I experienced as said throughout this book. Now that that is out there, and known, let's get into it.

Part 1:

The Good Old Days and

Before

When you're an only child, your youth is very different compared to those who have siblings, because it can go two different ways, usually. With two or more children, in this case specifically, two – one is either favored (don't deny it, you know there's some truth to that statement), or the parents try, hopefully their hardest, to make absolutely sure that each child is treated with the same attention and love. With an only child, that's not the case. This may seem obvious, but in most cases, and I emphasize most, the only child gets all the attention and love. If not, there could be a multiplex of reasons why they aren't. Sorry, this isn't a parenting 101 book. Might I add, it could be perceived that I'm making children without brothers and sisters have the advantage here. Growing up, I never stopped hearing people tell me how lucky I was to not have any siblings, but trust me, it's not a luck thing. It was a bittersweet thing for me. I'm grateful every day to have parents who always provided me with everything. And reflecting on that, would I have taken a brother or sister? Of course, but I think my life would have been drastically different, and I don't like the idea of that.

I grew up in two different places, both being towns in western Pennsylvania. Originally though, I lived in the town that we'll call Maca. The first house, a town house, was in Maca Heights, a more rural part of the town, where we lived until I was four years old, a toddler. The second house was with my father's mother, my grandmother, with whom we had lived with for around a year, which is where I had made a few unforgettable friends during my time there, three specifically, and it was the best. But the funny thing is, is that we were, and still are, the "only child" in our household. Seems almost like it was predestined to me. Four kids that become friends, who just so happen to all be only children? Come on.

See, when you have a brother or sister, you have someone around you all the time, mainly at a young age, but when you're an only child, you don't have anyone besides your mother and father. So, ideally, it was perfect growing up with other kids I could relate too, subconsciously, of course. If I knew that then, I'm not sure if I would be writing the same book.

The three kids from Maca were my absolute best friends. You know, those friends you had when you were just an innocent child, just wanting to constantly have fun. It wasn't complicated; three kids met in pre-school, and became best friends, simple. Well, this was until, eventually, my parents and I moved to a not-so-far away neighborhood in which we were building a house, in a neighborhood right outside of Ashbrook, Pennsylvania, we'll call it, where it was oh so different compared to living in Maca. Mainly, every friend I made where I had moved was merely a thirty-second bike ride away. Not that my three friends from Maca weren't as close, but this was different. It felt more akin to something I would see on T.V. about kids in the same neighborhood, riding bikes, knocking on doors to come outside and all. It just felt different. Maybe it was because I was a year older. Who knows. Anyways, most kids in the neighborhood were my age, so it was ideal for a loner like me. I still kept in touch with my friends from Maca, as they were a huge part of my childhood, but it was different with the kids in my new neighborhood. This would be the place where not only I would grow, but my mother, father, and I would grow as a family.

I still remember the day that we were fully moved into the house in Ashbrook. It was the second to last house in the cul-de-sac, a big, red brick house with an attached garage on the left, with a steep, longish driveway, and a black front door to the right that was covered by a mini-roof. It had plenty of windows that were surrounded by navy blue shutters, and a front yard that was excellent for sledding when it snowed in the winter. Most importantly, my room was above the front door, so I could see the entire cul-de-sac. The very first day we were officially moved in (as in able to sleep there that night), I vividly remember seeing a kid walking down the street to my newly-moved into house, who was wearing a bluish jacket and snow boots. It was summer, mind you. The kid was shorter than me, and a little husky. Before even telling me his name was Chuck, he asked me the same thing he would continue to ask for years to come, "You wanna play?" We became decent friends soon after that, but eventually, he had introduced me to his group of friends that had lived throughout the neighborhood. And as for the first time Chuck and I met and his perfectly out of season outfit choice, well, let's just say he had a particular personality, even at that age. That's just how I remember him. Being the new kid in the neighborhood, seeing someone your age walk over to to you to see if you want to play – you don't forget something like that. Or maybe I just wouldn't forget something like that, I'm not sure.

As the years went by, I became better friends with that select group, eventually really good friends with a few. All of the times we played baseball, kickball, any sport you can play with a few kids, we did it in the cul-de-sac of our street, or somewhere else in the neighborhood. All of the times that we played video games, or played a game called release when it got dark outside.

Everything we did contributed to me having an amazing childhood. To be honest, I believe if it wasn't for the friendships I had with those kids, and a few other best friends I have had throughout my entire life, my parents' divorce may have been a lot more difficult to cope with. For now, though, let's continue with the story.

Going backwards for a bit here, my mother had been good friends with her boss at her profession, which was and still is a hair stylist (more like hair artist). Ultimately, I was introduced to her boss' son, Jack, who was exceptionally outgoing and a lover of all things reptiles. He was certainly a wild one, but in all of the best ways possible. In turn, I became best friends – brothers even – with Jack, and still am. Alongside Jack, I was also best friends with another kid I had met in school, the first grade actually, who I would also call my brother to this day, his name was Arnold. Unlike Jack, Arnold was more quiet, but man, he always made me laugh, and he still does. Funnily enough, I still recall the one time that Arnold got sick, and didn't come to school. Our teacher asked if anyone knew where Arnold was, and I proudly answered that he had strep throat, which I always considered the start of our friendship. That's just how I remember it. Both Jack and Arnold were about the same age as me, five or six, when we met. But going back to Jack – every year, from around age nine to age seventeen, our moms took us to Mexico, with the exception of a year or two. It was one year going to Mexico where I began to view my parents' relationship in a different light.

The first trip we went to Mexico, a place in Playa Del Carmen, my father did not accompany us. At the time, being as young as I was, I had no idea why. Although I do remember asking myself, and my mother why my dad was not going on vacation, out of the country, with my mom and I. I do not necessarily remember being told why he didn't go, either, and if I was, I felt like it might not have been the actual reason why, at least at first. But who knows. The next Mexico trip later, when I was around ten, I stopped thinking too hard about it. Coincidentally, it was during this period in my life when I noticed my parents' arguing became a concrete, reoccurring thing. Of course they had arguments before, as do all relationships, but it seemed as though something felt distinctive about these reoccurring arguments, almost like there was more genuine frustration than before, purely from the sound of their voices. It wasn't daily, or even weekly, but over time it became more frequent. My parents have argued in the past, but not this much. It wasn't violent arguing, or red-faced screaming, but it was definitely voices-raised exchanges. Maybe it was because I was becoming more self-aware, getting older and all, I just remember the arguments happening more as I got older. I do want to also add, the arguments were rarely directly in front of me. If they were going to argue, they did so in private, most of the time at least. Regardless, whether they knew it or not, I could usually hear it. I just couldn't help but listen. So I began asking myself again whether it was because of me, or not. If I was the cause for all of the conflict. Did I do something wrong for this to happen all the time? Am I the reason for this? Am I bad? As a kid witnessing this, what seemed like a big change in my parent's relationship, of course that would run through one's mind; why wouldn't it?

Also, I have to get something out of the way here before any ridiculous thoughts get put out there, because I know they will indeed get thrown around and morphed like a ball of clay. This is a little disclaimer, if you will: there was never, NEVER, any physical abuse between my parents, or towards me. If they had to let something out, it was through words, not punches. The only things that were ever punched were a wall and a windshield.

For the time it went on, it wasn't constant fighting. There were plenty of times where my mother and father actually seemed like they had a legitimate, loving marriage, not just in public and in front of family, but in front of me. I imagined it was like that between the two of them as well. You can have your own opinion on that, but at the time, it made me happy, seeing them getting along, what looked like just enjoying each other's presence. I even remember watching movies in their master bedroom while my mom laid on my dad on the love seat, and he messed with her hair, and I sat on the big chair next to them. It still feels like that was just yesterday. Man, do I miss the sound of putting a tape into the VHS player, with the tape winding up and all. But there was one thing I did notice, though, that never happened through this period I'm talking about; I never really heard neither my mother nor my father speak the words, "I love you," to one another, at least from what I remember. There was sometimes the obligatory "I love you" when they were about to end a phone call between each other, but that seemed to be it. That's when I really started to question what was going on, because I said it constantly, and always got the same response back. I always, and still do, pay close attention to the little things like that. I don't remember my parents sharing those words with each other. Those three words have always meant a great deal to me, and to never hear them exchanged between the two people I love the most in this world, was disheartening.

Between, and perhaps even before the Mexico trips with my mother and friends, my father took me to a bunch of places as well, so don't think that this an absentee father case, because it couldn't be farther away from such a thing. My dad couldn't have done more things with, and for me. Ranging from things like coaching my baseball teams, to taking me to places like Wildwood Highlands (as of the end of 2019, rest in peace to that amazing place), to just spending as much time as he could with me, and believe this, it was more than enough for a kid. I was merely happy to purely spend time with my dad. I just appreciate the time I can spend with my parents, every second of it. Over time, there was something I had picked up on, though. On certain occasions, we would meet one of my father's friends at places, mostly places with a giant arcade or, basically places where I could have fun with my friends. I didn't think much of it, thinking, "it's just one of Dad's friends," but I felt the problem lay in who the friend was specifically: a woman that was not my mother. It's not that married men can't be friends with women that aren't their wives, but one can see why a situation of that sort could seem... confusing.

So, eventually, I started putting two and two together. Occasionally when I went out with my father, that friend would be there, and my mother would not be. During that time, it could have been perceived as coincidental though to a kid, because my mother worked long hours five to six days a week, and my father worked five days a week and got off work earlier than my mother most of the time. I remember this taking place sometime when I was between the age of nine to ten years old.

Maybe it really was my father just taking his kid to have some fun, while also meeting up with a friend, especially considering that it wasn't always just my father and his friend that was that woman; we met plenty of his other friends places at times too. And maybe I was naive, but I really do think it very well was just that, two friends meeting up, and I just happened to be along with them. Things started to seem different on our next vacation.

Part 1.2:

The Course of the Divorce

In 2003, when I was about nine years old, my father and I drove to Cedar Point, although it wasn't my first time going there, as I went with my mother and my grandmother two years prior, this was the first time my father and I were going on a vacation together, just the two of us. Now, I don't remember the exact reason why my mother was not going with us, but after we got to a certain point on the drive there, I had a suspicion as to why my mother was not there.

Driving from the western Pennsylvania area to Sandusky, Ohio, to go to *Cedar Point* always required at least one break a little more than halfway through the road trip at a rest stop. I can still smell the combination all of the different fast food places, that french fry smell mixed with the cheesesteak aroma. This specific stop turned out to be different though. As we arrived in the parking lot, I saw two people get out of a car that happened to be parked next to us, a mother and her daughter. The daughter appeared to be young, possibly around my age. The mother, a tallish woman with blonde hair, brown eyes, that had a slightly upward, askew smile. The daughter had almost the same features, but dark hair, and missing the smile. I heard my father talk to the mother, and I got out of the car and saw that it was my father's friend from the previous few times we went places together. From here, we'll refer to my father's friend as Ellen. Keep in mind, this was not the biggest deal to me, because despite my father being with one of his friends on our trip, it didn't affect our time together; it just meant sharing it with two other people. Of course my father and I stayed in a separate hotel room than Ellen and her daughter, at the old Hotel Breakers specifically, and I do recall us walking around together occasionally, but not riding the rides together. All in all, the three days that my father and I spent at Cedar Point were amazing, and I loved every second of that time, especially considering I had an obsession with theme parks and roller-coasters, so don't go thinking that the short vacation was tainted. That's all I cared about in the end, spending time with my dad, even if he, still to this day, has a fear of riding roller-coasters, at least the more daunting ones. Motion sickness medicine was a good friend of his a few times on the trip.

Sadly, this is what gave me the final realization that everything truly could have been okay *between* my parents, or at the very least, something was off. I reiterate almost the same question that I did when I went to Mexico and my father didn't go, why didn't my mother come with us? I wanted her to be there.

Some time went by, and it was now the month when my mother had taken me to Mexico with our friends, her boss and Jack. But, yet again, my father didn't accompany us. In my mind at the time, I had a vague notion as to why he was not going with us, or why my mother didn't join us in Cedar Point, but I knew it wasn't the whole story. It couldn't have been. I thought maybe my mother and Ellen just didn't get along. I didn't see the real issue with it. It turned out that, or at least from what I can remember, Ellen did not want my father going to Mexico with us, and despite that fact baffling and confusing me, I can see why now that was the case. I'm not going to insinuate anything by tossing any terms out there. But, whether anything did occur or not is irrelevant at this specific point, because the person we went to Cedar Point with was not my mother. Although, yes, I had an absolute amazing time with my father, I just wanted to go away with both of my parents, together, as a family. Ellen was not part of our family. It seemed like the times we went away with just the three of us started to become a rare thing, considering the the last vacation we had taken together as a family of three was in South Carolina some four or five years previous to Cedar Point with my father.

My mother and I came back from Mexico, and things were back to the way they were, both parents acting as if everything is normal. That may sound shady, but it wasn't to me, because even with everything that was happening between my parents, my mother and father just wanted to make sure I was a happy kid, but eventually, putting on some sort of performance isn't healthy for anyone. An act can only go on for so long, before it becomes something else entirely. Bear in mind, ever since I was little, I have always been able to read my parents really well, always seeing when something might have been irking or bothering them. Listen, my otherworldly psychic talents aside, putting away feelings and important thoughts in front of kids just to serve one purpose is not always the way to go, and I know my parents realized that fact, but this is a family after all, and it's not always easy to make those decisions. That might be the go to answer at first, but eventually, that act will get old. I'm in no way saying fight and scream in front of the kids, or that parents need to share every single thing they are feeling with the kids either, but you shouldn't be afraid to have civilized conversations about your feelings.

On the exterior, things still appeared to be normal during this time. My father was coaching baseball with my mom cheering us on in the bleachers, we still went to dinner as a family as we always have, and we got along greatly, as a trio; however, now I know the building underlying tension between my parents, but I hid it away, which, in certain cases, particularly this one, was *mostly* the right move. It caused my parents to keep the entire situation between them and them only, and not unnecessarily bring their kid into it because it wasn't about me; it was about a husband

and a wife figure out their relationship. Maybe I felt that I wasn't ready to share that I had an idea of what was going on. Looking back on that fact, as a kid, I believe I was too young and scared to have even mentioned anything to them at that point, but if I had, I'm not sure it would have been the right thing to do anyways. As an older version of myself looking back at the situation, I of course believe that I should have maybe mentioned my feelings to a different degree. Yet, I wouldn't have to say anything at all.

At this point in time, I was eleven years old, and we have now reached the point where the arguing was at a critical point. I noticed that when the arguing did happen, it was on a much bigger scale than before. This is when the walls started getting punched, voices and tension seem to be raised to an all-time high, basically, the true indication that it was the downfall of my parents marriage from my point of view. I do need to reiterate that there was not many explosive arguments in front of me, and if there was, there was at least some kind of effort to keep the swearing and wall punching to a minimum. My parents kept that between the two of them. This is crucial, because doing so in front of your kids just leaves them a little more broken inside every time it occurs, seeing their parents act that way, especially towards each other. Not to say the kids won't get over it, because they eventually should (no guarantees folks), but at a certain age, or any age, depending on the person for that matter, it could essentially hurt them, and cause their minds to run wild in a negative way.

This is also the period where I have difficulty in remembering what happened in my pre-divorced parents' relationship. I'm not sure if it was because I ignored what was going on, or if I merely blocked it out. Maybe it's because I was truly hurt at that time, seeing my parents grow farther and farther apart. The point I want to make here is, if I wouldn't have subconsciously locked that stuff away, the story I am telling could have been very different here. I also spent boat loads of days and sleepovers with Arnold, who I had mentioned earlier. Starting to see a little trend here? I'm not saying you need friends to get through divorce as a kid, but the fact that I still have those two amazing souls that are Jack and Arnold in my life today should tell you the importance of having someone to help let go of the serious stuff for a while, at least as an only child. Hobbies especially help as well, and trust me when I say that film and video games also played a big part in my mind staying healthy. Some people might have a negative opinion on those hobbies, but to me, no matter the hobby, if it will help you – not escape, nor rely on, but cope – with what is going on between your parents, it'll work. For me, a good mix of friends and hobbies helped immensely. This is also why having brothers or sisters when your parents are going through something like a divorce is different compared to being an only child. Siblings have the chance to rely on each other in trying times, they have a shoulder to cry on. Only children do not have that. Siblings or no siblings, divorce is still divorce, and as long as you have something to smooth over the bumps, it can help a lot.

I will say that one of the few things I do remember, is that during this time, my parents didn't sleep in the same bed for a while, and yes, I know some happily married couples that have been together for a long time don't sleep in the same bed either, for a plethora of reasons, but in my parents' case, it felt like they just could not stand to be that close to one another, at least that's how I saw it. That's what I felt. It was a metaphor for their marriage. And there are parts of me that wish I could recall more from that period just for memory and nostalgia sake, and so I can proceed to entertain you with it, but I cant, so I'm going to skip forward just a few months, to when the situation between my parents seemed to head towards the direction that every family dreads. It happened so fast, just like life itself does.

I was twelve at the time, so in my head, I wasn't a little kid anymore. I could see it before the conversation even happened, the one that my parents were going to drop on me. Not, "the talk," but the other, one. The one that was going to break it to me. The fact that the two most perfect people, in my eyes, were splitting up. Getting divorced. At that point I was just waiting for some kind of discussion to occur between my parents and myself. Funnily enough, I briefly remember that conversion, but more importantly, the look on my mother's face as she told me what was happening. That worried, but reassuring facial expression my mother gives after she says the word 'awe,' as she raises her lower lip into her upper lip. As well as the look on my father's face, as he looked away with that anxious feeling I could, and still, see in his face today. Eyebrows tensed up and all. The talk was another thing I wanted to just black out forever, and I did I fine job I think, because I still can't remember where it happened. Maybe it was in their master bedroom, the one I had mentioned earlier. But my parents' faces? I could never forget that. Both of my parents just looked so disappointed, not in me, but in themselves. A look that no kid wants to see their parents have, whether it's because of the kid or not. It's not a pleasant look to see. It was just what I had seen. There was this feeling of guilt floating throughout the air, and I felt that it came directly from me. I felt like I failed my parents as their child, in some way.

Now knowing what was about to happen, all I could and wanted to think about was the happy times we had together, as a family of three; Us. I remember a montage of memories just flying through my head, like the vacation we took to Myrtle Beach when I was about four years old, to the last Halloweens and Christmases before things turned sour between my parents. The times we went to dinner at a beautiful, cozy restaurant in Maca before I had started kindergarten, where I would order my very own shrimp cocktail, a salad with lettuce, croutons and a side of ranch, and a filet. Of course, I would never finish all of it. Or watching *X-Files* when I was really young, while we ate beef stroganoff (we called it, and still call it noodles and meat) out of those black and white, ceramic bowls that had calla lilies on them.

And of course, I couldn't forget to add one of the most important things in my life, when my father brought home our one and only dog on my ninth birthday. Her name was Raven, a black Miniature Pinscher that was the runt in her litter, who's birthday was only a month before mine. Raven was almost like a beacon that represented a time when we were all happy together. She was the fourth member of our family. Some kids had brothers and sisters, I had raven.

To tell you the truth, I felt like I could probably fill an entire library of books with the good times we shared together, my parents and I, which was something else that kept my mind together. I think they still do keep my mind together.

Happy memories.

I feel like most of the time, considering the purpose of this book, there will always be a yin and yang to situations like this, a balance of good and bad, but sometimes the bad can outweigh the good. The reality is, one has to deal with it one way or another. So, in my case, I tried to make the most of it, spending as much time as I could with the both of my parents, together, while I still could, because I had no idea what was going to occur next. Something we all knew though, was that my parents' marriage was over. Although, some salvation was attempted, and occasionally, things started to seem ebullient, but of course, the attempts were futile. At least they tried right? Although I still struggle trying recall this time in my life, most of what I do remember of this transformation period, was playing baseball (and hitting the ball over my mother's head in the stands after she told herself that I would), spending time with my parents, playing video games and hanging out with friends. And of course, I can't leave out having Raven by my side to help me stay as positive as I could. Ah, the times we used to give her a bath, just to watch her run Mach 5 around the house after she was done.

I do remember it feeling like the countdown to the end of the world, the escalation of my parents' divorce, just trying to live and be as happy as possible before it all goes out of the window. Gone.

To be honest, regardless of how comfortable or accepting I am with everything, it was never a period of time that I cared to remember that much, at least the bad stuff, mostly because I knew it was over. I still get that butterfly feeling in my stomach – the one you get at night before an anxiety-inducing next day – when I think of this time, specifically because as of a twelve year old kid, it was the day the world didn't end, but was about to change forever.

I woke up one morning – it was a dreary, cold Sunday, (it is western Pennsylvania, of course it was dreary) – to the sound of a truck running outside, and you might have guessed it; lo and behold, it was a moving truck. I look out my parents' bathroom because that was the easiest window to view the driveway without actually going outside, and see things are being loaded onto the truck: furniture, a television, basically all of the things that I knew my mother would probably take. She was leaving. It felt like the day of a funeral in a movie. I can still smell the fumes of the running truck.

The day I had dreaded coming, was here, and at the time, it was scary as all hell to me, because, well, what next? I had some dreadful questions in my head. I'm going to see my mother again, right? Where am I going to keep my stuff? Do I take it back and forth? What am I going to do? What – about – me? I remember constantly asking both of my parents what I could have done to stop whatever was happening. Asking if a hug could help, or a mere few words. Nothing worked. Hope was absent that day.

Now, it may appear that this happened awfully quick, and honestly, it did happen that fast, especially being the age I was. It was like a bad bolt of lightning struck and that was it. I mean, the day before the moving truck was in my driveway felt like any other day in the Thein household to me, and the moving truck day was the final nail in our household's coffin. I felt blind-sided, waking up to that, even though I knew the time would eventually come.

Before my mother left, she asked my father one last thing before driving away in the moving truck, "There is absolutely no way we can save this?" My father replied with, "Nope," and that was it. That was the end. No more husband and wife, no more mother and father living under the same roof. Most importantly though, no more trio. It would be two separate duos, at least, for the time being.

I gave my mother a hug and kiss, and she followed with, "I love you buddy. So much. I'll call you later."

Part 1.3:

And Everything Else After

As a kid, when your parents get divorced, it almost feels as if your life is, quite literally, splitting in two, becoming two different things entirely. Following the day one of the two parents moves away, arrangements either happen before or follow, that decide where the kids spend their time and on what days. That's what it was like for me, at least. Some arrangements consist of only one house, where the mother or father visits from time to time during the week. Other times, the kids go to the opposite house on the weekends. In specific cases, sometimes the kid is forbidden to even see the other parent. Obviously if you have divorced parents, you will already know this. But, my case was different. For what the situation was, it seemed to be a reasonable compromise between my parents, and as long as I got to frequently see both of them, it was a reasonable compromise for me as well.

Considering my mother's long and strenuous work schedule, my entire living arrangement stemmed off of that schedule. For example, she usually worked Monday through Thursday, most days until nine p.m. This created those living arrangements for what would be the next ten years of my life, and although it has switched from time to time, it was based off of the same criteria for all of those years.

So, my schedule went accordingly: Monday through Wednesday, I would be with my father and Raven; Friday through Sunday, I would be with my mother; Thursdays would be switched every other week. At first, it seemed pretty hectic for me, because it was something I definitely was not used to doing, going back and forth constantly. Unless you've done it, it's hard to really explain the new feeling of traveling between two different houses every few days as anything but confusing at first, and then becoming tiresome later. I – nay, we – made it work, because we had to, and these were the circumstances we would have to work with for a long time. Even if I had to take my stuff (when I say 'stuff,' I'm not speaking about clothes, I'm talking about things like movies I wanted to watch with both parents, video games, and my school stuff) back and forth with me between houses two times a week, it didn't matter. I didn't care because I would get to see my mom and dad every week, regardless of where I had to go to do so.

Not long after the moving truck day, we successfully relocated into my mother's new place, a sizable townhouse in a fairly pleasant neighborhood, while my father remained a mere ten minutes away in the house my parents had built seven years prior in Ashbrook. To be honest with you, yes, it was bizarre at first, having *two* houses to call home, but after getting warm to it, my mother's house was just as cozy as my father's, and that was the most peculiar part. Not having my father live in the house was a significant change, of course, but right before my mother moved out, my parents did not speak to each other as frequently as other married couples, sleep in the same bed, or basically do anything a couple does together, so I was already partially used to that fact. Even then, it felt unnatural at first, waking up at my mother's, going downstairs and only seeing my mother. No father in sight. It felt drab – depressing, even – knowing that as of that time, I would never wake up to my parents in the same house, ever again. It was so abnormal to me: all three of us not living, eating, or sleeping under the same roof. No matter the age when your parents get divorced – unless you were already living alone – warming up to that fact would take some time; at least it did for me. I remember the first time eating dinner at my mother's new place after the split, chicken breast and asparagus. What would normally be an extremely talkative time during the day, seemed post-apocalyptic to me. It almost felt like a desert wasteland after a bomb went off. Too quiet. Words were exchanged, but my normally outgoing mother wasn't herself, for good reason. And me, I was just so bewildered at how my family got to this point. Inside, I was just flat out sad. Overtime that quietness quickly changed into conversations about the situation, but I'll never forget what it was like the day after the move. It'll be imprinted in my brain forever.

So, the time I spent was split like I had mentioned above: Monday through Wednesday, I would be with my father; Friday through Sunday, I would be with my mother; Thursdays would be switched every other week; I remember it vividly. I was in middle school, so my mother would drive me to school on the days I was at her house. I would ride the bus home, sat in the first seat, and I would talk to no one on the way back. At my father's, which was still the house the three of us (and Raven!) had all once lived in, I would ride the bus both ways, as I had still lived in the house which resided in the neighborhood where some of my good friends still were. Despite that, I was more than comfortable with the situation at my mother's, so having a brief car ride every morning with my mother, instead of riding the bus, wasn't too distressing. I still don't know why I didn't ask her to just pick me up from school the days that she wasn't working, but whatever. Regardless of the entire situation, the main point is: this is probably the strangest stage in the whole divorce thing, 'this,' being the adjustment stage.

If your parents have never split up, I want you to imagine living under the same roof with the same people from the very first moment you can recall. For every moment you can remember, it would, and should, consist of living with those people. All of the dinners, the movies watched in the living room, the Christmases, the holidays; everything is spent together, otherwise known as being a family. (By the way, Christmas. I want to add that the whole, "I get two Christmases! More gifts!" thing is absurd, no matter. Forget the gifts. I just wanted to spend Christmas with both of my parents. One tree, in the same house, with one dinner.) Now, imagine that being stripped away from you, and you're thrown into two different places. Obviously, something is missing; something crucial is missing that completed the formula of all of those heartfelt memories that reside in that one part of the brain associated with remembering that hilarious thing that happened with the tree and the star with your father last Christmas. It's an empty, unfair feeling, one that someone experiences when they know that something isn't the way it should be, but in that moment, cannot be fixed. They must live with that ostensibly unsolvable problem, that they'd die to solve, but can't. That was how I felt during the first Christmas as a broken family.

At first, this altered, new world may seem confusing to you with a major change like that, while at the same time, everything continues on normally, just as it would if that person who left, was still there, because here's the thing: that person is still your mother or father, and they don't love you any less, and that will never change. This is one thing that must be accepted from the very start of a divorce from the child's eyes. Life goes on.

You are still your parents' child, and just because their relationship is merely no longer bound by marriage, does not mean that your relationship with your parents has been literally defiled or torn apart. The relationship between you and your individual parents is a complete, infinite fact that will never stray, or wander from its path, as long as you all do not want it too. So, with the acceptance of that in mind, your involvement in the trio relationship is out of the picture, and it should stay that way. The more the child tries to attempt to reignite a romantic flame that has now been completely extinguished, it becomes counter-productive, no matter the reason for the divorce. I mean, maybe there's some articulate, fifteen-year-old psychologist that can use a special method of mending their parents' relationship back together, but let's be rational here, I wasn't that. This was the time that had reinforced the idea that I'm not part of this dilemma, and that it was between my parents alone, until a new part of the plot was introduced: my mother started to see someone, that wasn't my father.

Part 2: Mom

My mother stayed in the same townhouse for about a year, until she decided to move in with her parents for a brief period, with plans to find a more convenient place for us to live compared to the last house. She wanted a place that felt more like *our* home. On the flip side, my father was also residing with his mother who was 88 or 89 years old at the time (who was living as strong as ever), because of complicated circumstances pertaining to the house we had previously lived in together, the one in Ashbrook.

Man, that house. It may not seem like a big deal to one that never moved from this location to that location as a kid, but leaving the house you grew up in, where you made unforgettable memories with your parents and some of your best friends, can hit you harder than a meteor hitting Earth. Thankfully, I still have those memories, and a house is just a place to live. It's part of growing up, adjusting to change.

Anyways, at this point, I was still going back and forth, staying at each house the same days as the previous year. As of this specific place in my story, only one detail is relevant, which I believe might hit home for some kids whose parents have gone through divorce. My mother started to see someone new, someone that was not my father. This man was in her life previously, long before she had met my father, who we'll call Marcus. Before even meeting this new man, when I had found out about him, I couldn't help but ask myself the normal questions for a kid in my situation, "Is he going to replace my father? No way, he couldn't be. Duh, Alec. Don't be ridiculous." I had to believe that my parents still loved each other, regardless of their situation; I wouldn't let myself think otherwise. So, how could this person I had just met, replace my father? He couldn't. So I redirected my thinking to, "what could it hurt," to let this new guy not only into my mother's life, but mine as well. It was obvious to me that this new thing would be a drastic change to our lives, but maybe it could be a good thing. And although I was going to go into this new thing completely open minded, I also had other feelings about my parents generally being with other people that were not each other. It cut deep. I hated it. That included when my father began formally dating his girlfriend as well, but we're saving that for later.

To me, my mother going on a date with someone new, meant that we were straying further and further away from the normalcy we used to have as a family. It would have been the same if it was my father dating a new woman that wasn't my mother. But I had to give it a chance. I thought, "let's just see where this goes." Hell, it could be a really positive thing, a new man, a new start. I had no idea how this would truly affect our lives, but I would soon find out.

For kids that have had married parents all of their lives, this might be hard to perceive, but think about it like this: at first, whether or not it's true, and it wasn't, it really does feel like your mom (or dad) is trying to replace the significant other, even when they're not. I must say, it was pretty confusing at first, continuing to ask myself stuff like, "What if I don't think he's good enough for my mom? Are they going to get married?" As a kid, the whole divorce thing was still a brand new world to me, even if I was used to our living arrangements by this time, it was questions like that that *would* have consumed me, but I didn't jump to conclusions in the end; never jump to conclusions in a situation like divorce, as you never truly know what is going on, without asking, when it's appropriate to do so. Sure, ask questions in your own head, but never assume anything. In this case, I felt it was appropriate to know what was going on, so I finally decided I wanted to meet the man my mom was dating. I knew it was important to her, so I made it important to me.

One weekend, while I was sitting in my room, which was my pap's spare bedroom at the time, playing some video game, which I believe was *Rock Band* (A music rhythm game, in which I was an absolute professional drummer), my mother knocked twice on my door, walked in, and there he was, in the reflection of the mirror behind my TV. I could smell the cologne before I even turned around. It was a man, about the same height as my thirteen-year-old self (around five foot nine inches), bigger than me, but still skinny, with jet black hair and a bright smile. He came off pretty brutish, but he seemed nice. Behold, my mother's new friend, boyfriend, whatever. So, I paused the song that I was playing, stood up, shook his hand firmly, and introduced myself, and he proceeded to do the same. In this story, we're going to name him Marcus. I remember the entire ordeal vividly, because something like this, one does not forget. From this moment on, Marcus would affect not only my mother's life, but mine as well.

It's amazing how time truly can fly by when things get into a groove, especially a good one. My mother had been officially dating Marcus for a while now, and my father had started dating his now-girlfriend who he had known for years. You know, the woman my father and I had went to Cedar Point with? So this whole, parent-dating-new-person thing, wasn't something too fresh, or new to me, mainly due to my mother and Marcus, but also partially because I had already known the woman for a decent period of time before my father and her were even a thing. But seeing my mother with someone I had never previously known before, well that was a different take for me. That's a good thing though, you need things to shake up your life, and these events did. My parents were already divorced, I had to give new things a shot.

During this period, everything was going great between the split parties of what used to be the trio my parents and I were a part of. My mother was getting along great with her boyfriend; my father was getting along great with his girlfriend; both of whom I enjoyed being around, despite the boyfriend and girlfriend not being my father and mother. I got through life just as I would have if my parents were still together, at least I believe I did. That's not to say that things wouldn't be different, for better or worse. I must add though, it took me a while to truly get used to my parents dating different people. I feel differently now, but looking back, it was...weird to deal with... at first. I wouldn't say I was or wasn't immediately accepting of it. Maybe not one hundred percent at the beginning, but after a few months of getting used to yet another new situation, I was more open to this new chapter in life. In the end, it didn't matter what I thought though, to me at least, because my mother was happy, or it seemed like she was to me.

My mother and father spent years taking care of me, even directly after getting a divorce. They spent her time making sure I was happy. It was time I tried to return the favor.

Things did start to change, specifically, for my parents, and myself. I could see it in my mother, as she had started wearing clothes (outside of work) that more or less complimented her boyfriend. They both wore specific clothing from the same stores most of the time. I'll say that she started to wear expensive t-shirts, jeans, and black boots more than what she had worn previously, which was more formal wear. There was nothing wrong with that, either. She was still herself. I liked that she had obviously found someone I thought she liked, because she was putting in effort. And me? I was growing to learn to live truly without my parents being a singular object, or item. Because I was getting older, those questions that I had asked myself before like, "Is he replacing my father?" were no longer even running across my mind. My mother was still my mother, and my father was still my father. That fact wouldn't change.

About a year later, my mom decided to move into a new house by herself, as in it wasn't with Marcus, but they were still very much together. It was orangish-pink, cozy, and minutes away from the school I had attended for the past 4 years (the middle school and high school were directly next to each other). It was convenient, like she had been looking for. In my opinion, this was the time when some of the true colors of the boyfriend started to show. At this time, I didn't drive yet, so my father would still drive me back to my mother's house when our time for the week together had ended, enter the house with me, say hello and give a "How are you?" and "How was work?" to my mother, give me a hug and a, "I love you. Call you later, Buddy-man." Mind you, even though it was more than civil before, the relationship between my parents during this time started to reform itself, I felt, though not the same relationship when they were together, but something new. It felt more like good friends. I could really feel it, or merely see part of it coming back together. It didn't feel like a ruse, or a show, as there was no reason for that. It felt real, and my oh my did it make me happy. Of course, it was a double-edged sword.

On one particular day, Marcus was at my mother's house, and was waiting in the driveway, smoking a cigar in the driveway, when my father and I had pulled in. I got out of the truck, and Marcus said, "What's up?" I gave him a nod and a quick "What's goin' on, man?" and stood by the door, waiting for my dad to walk in the house with me to say hello to my mom. Marcus put his cigar out, then walked up to my dad's red truck, and started talking to him. Just as a background, Marcus and my father talked many times before this, and were perfectly cool with each other. It was a decently civil relationship, and Marcus knew that my mother and father were friends, before this upcoming talk had occurred. More than enough words were exchanged to establish a fairly normal conversation, although there were a few words which, to this day, still render me surprised, and aggravated. Marcus said to my father, something along the lines of, "Listen, I don't want you coming in the house anymore. She (as in my mother) isn't your wife, so I would appreciate it if you just dropped Alec off and left from now on. This is getting ridiculous. You don't need to come in the house every time you drop him off. You know what I mean?" Now, my dad has always been an extremely generous, understanding person, but used to have a particular inner temper that could lash out if something hit him the wrong or right, way, but that was very rare. When I heard Marcus giving him this demand or order, rather, I thought this could be one of those rare times for my father. Well, to my surprise of Marcus telling my own father that he could not come into my house, nothing happened. It wasn't even a conflict. My father merely said, "I can respect that. No problem, man," and that was the end of it. No mention of it between the two again. I honestly don't think they spoke for a very long time after that. My father truly respected his wish. It was also proof that my father changed. Deep down, I personally wasn't having it, but considering it was my mother's boyfriend, I held back my tongue for a while out of respect for her. So what was I to do? Marcus made my mother happy, so saying something to him might end up upsetting her. The conversation between the two men, the father and the boyfriend, became a thing of the past, as all things do. So I left it be.

A week or so later, when Marcus wasn't there, I do recall my mother asking my father why he wouldn't come in when he dropped me off one day, and he answered honestly. My father told my mother that Marcus did not want him in the house. The 'rule' that Marcus had set with my father had quickly dissipated.

I eventually got used to Marcus being around, and more importantly, him being with my mother. I was in high school at this time, and still had two years left until graduation, so I had a lot of time to get to know Marcus, and to be honest with you, he grew on me for the most part. Besides the fact that he would take my mother and me to different places all the time, treat me with a fair amount of respect, there were two things that he did right. First, Marcus actually made the attempt to get to know me, which I can appreciate. And secondly, he treated my mother with plenty care and affection. As most people know, relationships can be complex, and of course, love can be an extremely slippery slope, and eventually Marcus started to slip.

There was one thing I hadn't seen, or at least known about Marcus for the longest time, that man had anger issues. Sure, he came off brutish and stern at times, but I thought it might have just been his exterior. Although I was too young to go out for drinks with my mother and Marcus, I recall hearing more than a few stories some years later of Marcus getting intoxicated, and wanting to fight multiple people that looked at my mother, accidentally bumped into him, or apparently didn't do anything wrong at all. I also recall my mother telling me about the time Marcus tried to drag her and saying, "Let's go," out of a party at her friends' place, because he didn't want her there. This was while all her friends there were screaming at him until he had left. And that was after he had called her plenty of names that would make a child glow with anger. Listen, I'll reiterate here, I only wanted my mother to be happy, but hearing those kind of things are pretty hard to take and just brush off. This wasn't Marcus telling my father that he wasn't allowed in my mother's house, this was excessive and out of line.

Over time, I noticed even more particulars about Marcus that really brought out a few glimpses of his true colors, or his true self, more-so than before. Specifically, the time my mother and Marcus drove north for a weekend, and Marcus refused to take his car. He insisted on not only taking my mother's car, but driving it as well. So, upon returning from their trip, I awaited the two outside on the deck and had seen Marcus driving with my mother in the passenger seat. My mother walked out of the garage with a disgusted look on her face. I wasn't sure what to think, but I knew that look, something was obviously amiss. I walked into the house with my mother, and apparently Marcus hit something on the way home, damaging the bottom of my mother's car badly. My mother always considered the damage to be her fault, since she let him drive the car, putting all of the blame on herself, but that wasn't the point. The point was that Marcus broke something and felt it wasn't his responsibility to get it taken care of. Some may be thinking that those incidents aren't too harmful, and that Marcus is just a 'hothead,' or something. I thought the same thing, until we went on a little trip together.

Marcus, my mother, and I went to these rapids that seemed to take forever to get to. The trip started out excellent, considering it was my first time taking on rapids, and I was more than thrilled to get going on the river, with my once extreme-attitude towards life. The car ride seemed long, but I've always enjoyed road trips so I didn't mind. Though, suffice it to say, my attitude went from amped, to aggravated beyond comprehension. Considering white water rafting is a group effort, as far as what we participated in, there are always going to be people in the front, middle, and back of the raft on both sides, about seven people total, including the guide in the very front of the raft. So for our group, I was in the front on the right, my mother was behind me, and Marcus was next to her on the left (the rest were randoms in the group). As I previously mentioned, the trip started out great, as did the time on the rapids. It was exhilarating, even if it wasn't some death defying, raging water. It was amazing, well, until Marcus' impatience and "hotheadedness" seemingly started to kick in.

Regardless of the extremity, it was still white water rafting, so our group had to paddle as though our lives had depended on it, if we wanted to keep moving properly. At one point, Marcus seemed to be displeased with the effort he felt my mother was putting into paddling, so he proceeded to get audibly angry. Some fifteen minutes later, as we reached a slight drop, I recall hearing my mother looking back at my mother and saw what looked like Marcus hit her in the face with the back end of the paddle accidentally. I'm sure the two behind my mother and Marcus had seen what happened, although one did ask if she was okay. I know what I saw though: my mother with a semi-bloody mouth, obviously upset, I made sure she was okay, but since there wasn't much I could say to Marcus, given our situation, stuck in giant raft on raging waters and all, I didn't say anything. My recollection consists of my mother holding her mouth and saying, "What the hell is wrong with you?" and Marcus replying with, "Haha, what? You're okay." I can still see the slight smirk on his face to this day.

I don't remember much after getting off of the water, but I do recall the ride home being completely silent. The entire overly long drive home, consisted of thinking to myself what I was going to say to Marcus, and also thinking, "Maybe it was just an accident." I didn't end up speaking a word to him to the entire time.

When we had finally arrived at my mother's house, Marcus had dropped my mother and I off at our house and left. My mother and I proceeded to briefly talk about what had happened on the raft, mainly about how she could have fallen out drowned after being hit the face. Marcus hit my mother in the face with the paddle, and didn't apologize or anything. Nothing. I was done with him. Even besides the rafting incident, whether he was insecure, angry towards my father for being with my mother before he was (it was an actual thing), or just stuck in his fantasy of reliving his twenties, I didn't care what it was. The bottom line was that Marcus needed to be out of our life. Of course, the raft episode very well could have been an accident, and it probably was, but where's the sorry? Even if he had apologized to my mother without my knowledge, I would have appreciated an apology myself, for making what was at first a fun trip, turn sour. Maybe Marcus thought that wasn't his responsibility either. Now, one could probably correlate the things that happened to something like some intermittent explosive disorder, or merely alcoholism, but looking back, I personally don't believe it was, especially considering that half of the incidents seemed to occur when he was sober. I think Marcus was multiple, negative things that definitely required some form of help, and alcohol merely brought out the worst things in him, while already being bad to begin with.

The emotional distress became more prevalent shortly after our trip. Sure, there was the party Marcus tried to drag my mother out of, the confrontation with my father, the time Marcus damaging the bottom of my mother's car previously. Oh and I forgot to mention, trying to convince my mother to sell her old engagement ring my father had given her, so Marcus could buy a ring for my mother with the profit. Would I be mistaken to believe that all of those things would be considered red flags? Yeah, I think not. There was, maybe, one time where I felt Marcus really tried to have something of a relationship with me, without my mother's presence. He had taken me to breakfast one morning, trying diligently it seemed, to get to know me. I did appreciate the thought behind that. Basically, there was effort from Marcus, but it was too late. The bad outweighed the good. I had, and still have, more rotten memories of him than pleasant ones. I pretty much only remember him taking me to breakfast, as far as the nice thoughts go. Shortly after the rapids adventure, though, things started to change. My mother had started to grow apart from Marcus, as he started to show up at the pink house less and less. After a month or so of more unanswered calls than answered, my mother ended her relationship with Marcus.

My mother dated Marcus for a total of six years (yes, six years), before breaking up with him. There was even a planned 'ring' thing that was supposed to happen, which I mentioned previously. Even though I wish I could remember the details on how the break up went, I didn't care. Because no matter how everything turned out, Marcus was gone. He was out of our lives, along with the unwanted baggage and persona he brought along with him, and that was all that mattered to my mother and me. I know it may sound a little selfish or insensitive of myself to act like that, happy my mother's boyfriend of six years was gone. She put in many years of her life for him, and that's the saddest part, spending that much time with someone only for it to turn out as sour as it did. She deserved to spend that time with someone better. It's an upsetting thing. I don't necessarily forgive Marcus for what he put my mother through, but the past is the past, people make mistakes, and I try not to dwell on it.

One thing you always have to be ready for as a child of divorce, is knowing that once that first boyfriend, or first girlfriend is in and out of the picture, things become easier, in that regard. Not only because you're now used to your parent being with someone other than your mother or father, but also because you have an easier time looking out for certain red flags that could prevent or at least assist in seeing the toxic burdens that one might not discover until it's too late.

Hopefully that first boyfriend or girlfriend is better than Marcus.

After Marcus was out of the picture, sure, I was suspicious of anyone my mom went out with. But after a date or so, I was far more optimistic, especially after hearing great things from my mother about the new guy she had been seeing. Henry, I'll call him. Henry was very tall and muscular, with blonde hair and some stubble on his face, and wore small, black rimmed glasses. And wow, he couldn't have been more different from Marcus. Classy, polite – honestly, he just felt like a refresh – anything did after Marcus was gone. Sadly, my mother and Henry only lasted some less than a year. Funnily enough, up until recently, as in a year or so, my mom's mother would constantly say how much she liked Henry, and asked if my mother had talked to him lately. I never heard my grandma ask if my mom talked to Marcus, at all. After that, my mother went out on a few dates with some other men, but no one really stuck.

Something I deeply regret, is not confronting Marcus, for all of the stress he put my mother through. See, I believe the partial reason why I went through the time with Marcus, without rebellion, is because not only does a child of divorce have to understand that this is inevitable, your parents seeking partnership with another person, but also that they need happiness too. In your parents' eyes, their goal specifically in this case, after a divorce, is making sure their kids are happy, and are raised well. I will admit, the main reason why I didn't rebel against Marcus, is because I was scared, or even cowardly. I was not only scared of him, that guy filled an absurd amount of rage and insecurity, but I was scared of taking happiness away from my mother. Isn't that what truly matters in the end? That everyone is happy? I didn't want there to be any chance of pushing my mother away from me, and closer to him, no matter how far-fetched that sounds.

Sometimes, the happiness that one shows can merely be a mask, and behind that mask could be someone that is blinded by affection, and the security of having someone in their lives. Because of that, I believe, you get my amazing mother, staying with Marcus for as long as she did.

Rewinding back to divorced parents' relationships for a second.

Once you accept that your parents are probably not going to get back together, it makes the situation with the pseudo-parents much easier to cope with. Now I'm not saying give up on the hope that your parents will *ever* get back together. That thought will always be in the back of your mind, that hope. That dream. I'm just saying, give something new a chance, as it will make life much smoother. Don't let yourself get stuck thinking about the negative things that occurred with your parents. Try to open your mind to new things, as in maybe this new person will make your parent the happiest person on earth. That worked for me (just in general. We're excluding Marcus here). I think of the positive things, like my parents' love towards me, despite their differences. You need to use that positive energy to keep going, as that energy will also help your parents. Because remember, it's not just about you when it comes to the divorce. Sure, it may be between the parents, but it's about everyone in the family. Everyone needs and deserves to be happy. There was a family there once, don't forget that.

If only the good stuff lasted forever.

Not long after my mother had ended things with Marcus, my great grandmother, on my mother's side that is, had started showing signs of her age. At least to me she did. To a normal person over 90 years old, I'm sure staying as healthy as possible isn't the easiest job in the world, with prescriptions, diets, and medical issues. Now, my great grandmother, being 96 years old, didn't look a day over 80. She wasn't much for the countless prescriptions and diets (for the most part). She ate what she felt like, which included a banana a day, might I add. I thought she was immortal, looking the same as she did in the years past. But, no one is immortal. Eventually, my great grandma started to change, as humans do.

I remember one of the first things I noticed in my great grandma that was abnormal, was when she had forgotten my birthday for the first time. It isn't a good feeling experiencing that, especially with someone that you are so close to. Being the over-analyst that I am, I started worrying. This was the woman who spent so much time with me as a little guy. All the countless mornings and afternoons she had babysat me when my parents were working; when I used to watch daytime television (Mister Rogers' Neighborhood and The Joy of Painting reruns, anyone?) with her while I played with the many toys she had gotten me; when my mother and I had lived with my grandparents, all those days she used to wait for me to get off the school bus, just to say hello to me and give me five dollars, even though I was more than happy to just see her. I didn't want the money.

The things one would never, and will never forget. So, because of the forgotten birthday, I had a feeling that the worst was coming. Eventually, my feeling was right.

A few months after my birthday in September, I believe it was around Christmas that year, my great grandma fell, and broke her hip. She spent a few days in the hospital, and my Pap decided it was time to put her in a home. Not too long after moving her, around three months, give or take, my great grandmother passed away. It was devastating to our family. It seemed like everything just happened in the blink of an eye. Considering we've never had the biggest family, we've all been really close to each other, and that includes my father. What I mean is, she meant the world to all of us, especially my Pap, her son of course. Without her, my childhood wouldn't have been remotely the same. My life wouldn't be the same. All in all, she did bless us with last one thing besides her love and all the amazing memories she left with us after passing: a new place to call our home.

At the time of my great grandmother's passing, my mother and I had still lived in the same pink house that we had lived in for the past three years. Growing tired of the pink house, I believe it was my Pap's and mother's decision to completely redo the interior of my great grandmother's house. It would be a challenge, due to most of the house, including both garages, one attached, one by itself, the wiring, pipes, etc, (pretty much everything besides the foundation and structure), were all at least 45 to 55 years old, a total redo had to be done. It would be a task, bearing in mind that they did not want to spend a fortune on reworking the house. Because my Pap has some serious skills with pretty much everything, we decided to hire my very good friend's father to do the dry wall, new front porch, and some other things, while we took care of the rest. While we were redoing the house, my mother and I lived in my grandparents' house right next door, now for the second time. I actually enjoyed it, to tell you the truth.

To take you back a bit, in 2013 (otherwise known as the time my mother was still with Marcus), around the same time that my great grandmother had passed away, my mother's mother had a pretty severe stroke. I'm not sure if both were a coincidence because of each other, but as you can see, the end of 2013 was a scary time. Even thinking about it as I proceed to type this out gives me heart palpitations.

I'll never forget the day I got the call from my mother, her telling me that my grandma had a stroke. Sitting at her table, tensing up, and then just completely losing control of her right side. I remember waiting at the hospital for a good while just to see her, and when I finally did, she couldn't speak. She couldn't even open her eyes most of the time. I spoke a few words to her, telling her how much I loved her and how I was right there, her only reaction was merely a couple blinks. I wasn't even sure she could hear me. The entire time I was there, I had that nervous feeling in my stomach. That could have been it for her. But, although she still doesn't have as much movement in her right arm as she did before the stroke, she's still to this day doing well. The weird thing about this entire situation, between my great grandmother's passing, and my grandma having a stroke, is, it's almost as if my mother was supposed to live next door to her parents after all this time, not to specifically take care of them, but just to be near them, and be there for them.

Since renovating the interior of my great grandmother's house four years ago, my mother still resides there, allowing us to assist and spend time with my grandparents everyday. Anytime my Pap needs help cutting the acres of grass, or my grandma wants my savory, Cajun scallops for dinner, we're right next door. I understand to some that may seem like sort of difficult, but not to us. We've been more than fortunate to spend time with them that we will never get back. The house was a blessing in many ways, not only for my mother and me, but as you will soon see, for someone else as well.

Part 3: Dad

While my mother continued her life in a separate house from my father, before everything with Marcus, my father was with that one familiar woman I had seen a few times growing up, mostly notably, the one we met with at Cedar Point, Ellen. Right after my mother moved out of the house, my father and I stayed in the house my mother, father, and I had lived in, the one in Ashbrook, for about another year after their divorce. It was during that year I guess you can say that my father and Ellen were officially an item, at least in my mind they were.

After that year went by, and my father planned on moving into his mother's, my grandmother's house. In actuality, it was somewhat depressing for me, because I had to leave the neighborhood where most of my good friends resided at the time, and where I made countless, incredible memories. When I look back to my childhood and where it was, that house and that neighborhood are what immediately come to mind. That place meant a lot to me. But it was out of my control, like most things in life, so I said my goodbyes to the house, and moved on, for the most part. I would see my friends from Ashbrook everyday in school, so I wouldn't be missing them too much, even though it would never be the same. It was the house that I would miss, and honestly, still miss to this day, but that could be just nostalgia talking.

At the time, my father moved in with my grandmother because my father needed a place to stay while he found a new place to live. It didn't matter to me where my father lived, as long as he was happy, had a chance to regroup, and I could see him. My father moving in with my grandma was actually a huge positive, as I had always loved her house. It felt like a new start, as it did when my mother moved as well. Well, it felt like a new start with the exception of my father's current girlfriend, Ellen. That was the one thing, regarding my father and my relationship, that felt like something from a different era. Either way, I was fine with it. My dad was happy, so I was.

For a reference of time, the move with my father happened a year after I started middle school, which was a year after my parents had split and my mother moved out. This was going to be the first time living away from the kids I had shared a neighborhood with for the first time in seven years. I didn't want to leave that neighborhood, but it wasn't my choice. Even with that being said, I was excited for the future, for some change. I met new friends, kept a few old ones, but life was great. The places I lived, my father's girlfriend, Ellen, everything remained the same for the most part. For the first time in a while, there was some consistency in my life, with both parents. I had been getting as serious as one could about playing baseball at the time as well, and I must say that I was grateful to always have both of my parents attend every game that I played.

I want to add that, being a child of divorce, it's difficult to not let the splitting of your parents affect your day to day life, and school is included in that. Growing up, school can be arduous already for some kids, and having your parents get a divorce during that time can just add to the stress. Though, it doesn't matter what age you are, it'll hit in some way, shape, or form. It's hard to focus on anything but that. For me personally, when the divorce first happened, it was all I could think about. So many different emotions ran through my mind every day, form pure frustration, to what felt like despair. It's not okay to keep that stuff tucked away. Listen, what I mean to say is that it's critical to talk about everything with your parents regarding the effects a divorce can cause, especially when one can't stop thinking about it, or anyone for that matter. I remember even making the attempt to talk to my middle school's guidance counselor, which proved to not help at all, although it was good to at least try. That also isn't to say that it won't work for someone else, so I do believe that it could be worth a shot. So, regardless of distractions, and the eventual transmogrification of negative emotions into positive ones, I made it to the end of what adults used to say, was supposed to be the best time of your life, right on time: graduation.

After I had graduated high school, I decided to pursue a music career, in which I was lucky enough to have both of my parents support me in that. Because of that, I was always home. During that time, it was becoming clear to me that my father was ready for a change, regarding his love life that is, especially considering the talks he had with me about no longer being happy with Ellen. Whether it was him getting bored with her, or being fed up with how he became less and less important to Ellen's life, which is ironic, considering how she never wanted my father to come on vacation with us. With these talks, that feeling of hope in the back of my mind and deep in my heart sneaked back up on me, and arose again that thought of my father and mother getting back together, even though I knew that at this point, come on – it was more than a long shot. Despite that, my father ended it with Ellen, and almost immediately seemed like a revitalized man. I recall my father talking to Ellen for a about a week every once in a while after they had split, but after that, he wanted nothing to do with her. It was obvious to me that my dad just wanted a complete fresh start. He pursued hobbies that he could not particularly get into much with Ellen, and even began cooking professionally, which he attempted to start towards the end of his relationship with her. Nonetheless, there was especially one hobby that he seemed to participate in briefly at times with his now ex-girlfriend, but it was only a once in a blue moon kind of activity: gambling.

Some time after breaking up with Ellen, it

was a year after I believe, give or take a few months, my father started going to the casino more than usual. At first, I thought, "Man, he must really be making some money," while also thinking, "Jeez, he better not have a problem." He did originally go because he's always loved the atmosphere, and he was just enjoying himself. He also used to go with his mom on occasion, but that's a story for later. Soon enough, I found out there was sort of an ulterior motive behind all of the casino trips; there was a woman there he had taken interest in, and honestly, I was ecstatic to meet her. It was something different; something that I truly thought would bring a new dynamic to my father's life other than being single, as well as to our relationship, and it did. It really made me happy, seeing my father excited to be with someone again, someone who wasn't his ex-girlfriend. Someone else, that was new. Admittedly though, even with my excitement to meet my dad's knew friend, part of me had an that inkling of hope that I would be going to meet my mom. I know, I know, that certainly isn't realistic to think at this point. It was naive or childish even, but that's just the way my brain worked. It was like that every time someone new found their way into my parents' love life. It was that thought that maybe the new person I was meeting was going to be...Hey! Surprise! It's mom! Or It's dad!

Of course, that hadn't happened though.

After a few weeks, I was finally able to meet my father's new girlfriend, who we will call, Valentina. Before I had met Valentina, I assumed before even hearing a single thing about her, that she must have been great, considering the way my father had been hyping her up. Soon after I had met her, I couldn't have been more right. I could see why my father seemed to be more chipper than usual, with Valentina being the polar opposite of who Ellen was. It was a something fresh, just as he was looking for. From the moment I met Valentina, she was high-spirited, with a big smile on her face and a pure sense of happiness to go along with it. She genuinely *looked* happy to meet me, which made the whole thing uncomplicated, adjusting to someone new.

Around the same time that I moved into my now-redone great grandmother's house, a few months before my 21st birthday, my grandma (my father's mother), now the same age as my great grandmother when she had passed away, started to get sick. Because of her age, and taking her house into account (the one that my father and I had moved into and had been living in for now eight years) had three floors, it was becoming increasingly difficult for my grandma to go up and down between three sets of stairs, so we had to hire temporary home care for her. She had adored that house of hers, so putting her in a place she didn't want to be was out of the question. My father couldn't always be there at the time to fully take care of her, and I went back and forth between my mother's and my father's house, as well starting my lovely adventure in attaining my degree, I couldn't always be at the full attention she would need.

With all of that being said, there was another, particular reason as to why we had hired home care. My parents, who now had been divorced for almost nine years, were planning on taking me to Aruba for my 21st birthday... together. Imagine seeing the two people who were once one, coming together to take their son on vacation for his birthday. It wasn't a quick family gathering, or a stop and chat while dropping me off at my mother's like in the past. It was a vacation. Sure, we didn't discover the root cause of divorce or something of the like, but to me, that felt like some sort of breakthrough when it came to the splitting up. Now, I knew my parents remained friends after they had split up, or had least rekindled a piece of something that once was, but this trip or event, was when I truly knew that my parents had overcome the stereotype that is divorce. I was proud then. I still am. My birthday could have been anywhere, that part is irrelevant here. The point is that the trio was back in one place longer than a few minutes, or a day, or even a week. Sure, it was my 21st birthday, but I was euphoric with the fact that my family was together, happy, for something longer than a holiday. Before that vacation, it was obvious to all of us that my family was different than others, but this was proof that divorce can be different, particularly in the long term, and healthy for the sake of everyone involved. Valentina, being kind soul that she was, my father's girlfriend, was okay with it too. She knew what the trip was: a birthday present given by parents to their kid. And me? If it wasn't already clear, I was absolutely thrilled. After all this time apart, I was going on vacation with just my mother and my father. I waited so long for it, and it the time finally came.

At this point, the thought of my parents getting back together had been lost somewhere in space, but this was refreshing, let alone downright enlightening. My mother and father had become so comfortable in their situation that they could take a week-and-a-half long vacation together. No fighting, no punching things, no clashing with a boyfriend, just pure fun with that trio that used to live under the same roof. And that wasn't the only thing that was different compared to nine years ago, nope. My parents were solemnly getting along better than when they were married. Just as a reminder, this was when I was attending an online college for a degree, so that was the only thing I had to truly "worry" about the entire time, nothing else. I was completely carefree. The trip was less stressing over something going wrong between my parents, and more, "What time are we going to the beach?" Not that I should have been worrying anyways. It was my 21st birthday, so most people would assume my first legal drink would be something I was looking forward to, and I was looking forward to it, but my parents and I being together was all I had wanted, and I had gotten it. That's the truth.

One could say it was a miraculous happening that was only specific to our family, and how most divorces can't go that smoothly, but I disagree. This vacation just proved, not only to me, but in general that divorce can be overcome by people putting in effort, and having the will to forgive. Imagine this though, would everything I had said previously have been possible if I, the son of my mother and father, was any less accepting of either parent after the divorce? No, it wouldn't have been. If I would have chosen a "side" (which would never happen, as even the thought of that is foolish in itself), this entire book would be blown out of existence. Being the child, and accepting what is going on between your parents is the first true step to a better divorce, and I will always stand by that thought. I do want to add that it is NOT the children's job to ensure that thought, though. It's up to the parents to help the kids believe that it will be okay. Without good parenting, and teamwork, the higher chance that the divorce will go awry. It's a team effort. Sure, there are cases of divorce that could very well be irredeemable, or at least appear so, but there's always a way to make things better for everyone. For us, the trip to Aruba was verification that we had an excellent relationship together, and I must tell you, it was great time. What about after the trip though?

Not too long after coming back from Aruba, give or take a month or two, my father and I started going to the casino together. We would go every once and a while, skip a few weeks, go again and so forth. It just became our thing to do together. Sometimes my grandma would go with us, and my dad would cart her around on her special blue, wheel walker. Most of the time we just took her to whatever group or section of slot machines she was interested in, and she would just walk around playing what she was feeling, with us checking on her every couple of minutes. Eventually, she could no longer walk to her full ability, at least without struggling or going slowly, so my father started putting her on the seat and pushing her around like her own, personal Chauffeur. Everyone at the casino knew her, since she was so sweet, and so outgoing towards the people around her, even if she did enjoy playing multiple machines at once. Soon enough though, that blue cart lost its brakes, and broke. So my father bought her a brand new, red one. She loved it, especially since she could now get around the casino a lot faster, safely. It was easier for her to play all the machines she wanted. My father's girlfriend, Valentina, had also become really close with my grandma, going to the casino with them, spending time with her when my father couldn't. It was almost like Valentina was meant to step into my father's life for this reason, among others. She treated my father's mother like her own.

After a while, about a year and a half later, my grandma got sick again, and I mean really sick. It would seem that brand new red wheel car wouldn't get as much use as we had thought. There was definitely something wrong. One late night, she had fallen trying to get our attention, or at the very early hours of the morning, and was yelling. Not because of the fall, but because she was in immense pain in her stomach. So, that night my father took her to the hospital. The next day, they found that she had a tumor in her stomach, cancer, of course. Grandma had complained about her stomach before, but this was obviously different, and serious. There had been mentions of an ulcer, but never anything like this. Over time, signs started to show that the tumor was growing worse, and was constantly bleeding. The doctors told us that it was bad and was only getting more severe. My father hired home care again, specifically the same worker that we had while my mother, father, and I went to Aruba, to come to the house every Wednesday to take care of her while my father and I were unable to do so. Because of the condition she was in, we could take care of her day and night, with the exception of Wednesday, since that was the only night my father and I went to the out occasionally. My grandma never liked staying in a hospital a second longer than necessary, so she was more than okay with having home care again. Even with the increased cravings in donuts and cookies she began having, we thought she was nearing the end.

Some time passed, and the inexplicable happens: my grandma's tumor had stopped bleeding, and was beginning to shrink, or at least that's what my dad said the doctor said. All I know is, she was getting better. Going from what we thought would have been terminal, went from what

I guess would be considered to be remission. It was a mystery to us, but a very welcome one indeed. My grandma had turned from being almost comatose, living in the family room of her house in a pseudo-hospital bed (with Raven by her side the entire time), since she wasn't able to go upstairs to her old bedroom, to being able to walk better again, and just felt more alive than she had in the past two years. This was especially obvious to us because, well, she couldn't wait to go out, and get to the casino again, to enjoy what was her hobby for the past few years. So of course we would take her whenever she wanted, as long as she was up for it. Truthfully, I still believe to this day, it was her pure will of wanting to live life as much as she could that kept my grandma alive longer. Whether it was the casino, sweets, or just being around family that did it, it worked. Personally, I think it was a mix of trying to outlive everyone, and the donuts, or my mother and grandma (my mom's mom) coming to the house to see her. Whatever it was, it worked.

As every day goes by in the my life, the more and more I wish the good times could just last indefinitely. With my grandma, just going back and reminiscing about that one Christmas my parents, my father's mother and I had at her house while we were living there. I remember wearing my little black leather jacket at one point and receiving a battery powered, toy motorcycle from Santa. I was five years old I think. I just remember how happy my grandmother looked the entire time.

The smile she wore lit up the room as much as the holiday lights did.

Well, after an added on, extraordinary seven months of life, the tumor started to grow and bleed again. One month later, it was clear that my grandma did not have long to live, as everything was getting worse. So, instead of staying in the hospital for her last few weeks, Grandma only wanted to stay in the house she had lived so long in, and had so many memories inside. My father respected that wish, of course, and his mom stayed in the house until the day that she passed away in March of 2017. That night will forever be branded into my brain; my father, his girlfriend Valentina, and I, as well as the nurses, were in the house taking care of her. She was asleep for mostly the entire evening, while on a painkiller. And while my father and his girlfriend eventually fell asleep, I awaited the inevitable. I even remember the nurses telling me that they might call me if she were to pass.

I ended up falling asleep around four o'clock in the morning, only to wake up to my father knocking on my door. He walked in, eyes red and full of tears, shaking his head. My dad said, "Ah, she's gone buddy. Grandma's gone." My Grandma had apparently passed away at around ten o'clock in the morning, holding Valentina's hand. And of course, Raven was sitting next to her the entire time, who apparently never had taken her eyes off of her. Sadly, it had happened when my father stepped out of the house for about ten minutes, and came back only to see that his mother, who had adopted my father around fifty-four years ago, (who he had truly seen as his one and only mother) had passed away. Despite our family knowing the time was coming, it was still harsh for us, as these things are, but that's just how things go I guess. There are some things that can be controlled, fixed, or rejuvenated, but death is inevitable, and my grandma had definitely lived life to the fullest for all 99 years of her life. I remember her getting angry with the local paper when it had stated another citizen of the town she resided in was the oldest living person in it, at 94 years old. She took pride in living that long, and I think if it were up to her, she maybe would have wanted to live for another 99 years. I think everyone that knew my Grandma would have wanted that too.

During the final days of my grandma's long life, my mother had been out of the country. I had to call and tell her of the news, and she said that at night, she felt something and heard a noise in the room she was sleeping in, as well as her friends' dog bark at something. There was nothing in the room. I'm not sure if that could be taken as a coincidence. They were always close, especially with my mother (sometimes with her mother as well, as they still believed each other to be family) coming down to my father's house to see her quite. It was almost as if she was saying goodbye to my mother who was almost four thousand miles away.

Believe what you want.

Part 4:

Time to Begin Again

With my grandmother's passing, came re-invigoration. A few months later, while still grieving, something was solidified, even more so than previously, the fact that my parents were best friends. My mother was always there for my father's mother, and my father was always there for my mother's parents. Basically, despite our family being small, everyone was always there for each other, even through the more tough times. So with that solidarity, the trio decided to take another trip, this time to Las Vegas. And despite my mother's general distaste towards going to the casino (but not gambling), we had an even more successful trip together. Mind you, this was my mother's idea for us to go together. I believe that we all felt, even more so than before, after my father's mother had passed that family should always be the most important thing in our lives. Without each other, divorced or not, where would we be? Us three being together, again no matter the location, further strengthened our relationship.

You know I enjoyed that, being with both of my parents on vacation again.

Coming home millionaires from Vegas or not (not), we became even closer than we had ever been before, and that includes when we were all under the same roof. Now, if that isn't grounds to have some sort of hope for your family, I'm not sure what exactly is. My father has been over to my mother's abode pretty frequently for holidays, as he has always had an open invitation, with the exception of when my mother was together with Marcus, of course. But it was clear now that everything was going better than it ever could. It just felt...heightened.

My grandmother (mother's mom) always used to ask me after the divorce if I was ever going to be okay, always trying to ensure that I wouldn't be scarred forever from such a terrible situation. The question was out of love, obviously. And harsh or not, her asking that question as frequently as she did is a testament to how people generally view divorce, this vile thing that ruins lives. Regardless, I always gave the same sort of honest answer every time she asked, "Grandma, I'm great." Because of the frequency the question was asked by her, I don't think she believed me, and I get it. I don't blame her for asking that. The process of divorce *can* vile, but it doesn't have to be.

As time passed though, my Grandma and Pap looked forward to seeing my dad just as much as me when he would stop over. Everyone knew that in the end, the divorce helped. And if you couldn't tell at this point, I never legitimately looked at my parents' divorce as a terrible situation, not even a bad one. It was just...there. Was it sad? Extremely. Did I like it? Definitely not. Did I eventually realize that it had to happen? Sure. Sometimes you have to go through the bad to get to the good. I have always seen that our situation was better the way that it turned out, even before it happened to completion, because I didn't put myself in front of what was trying to be worked out. I let my parents do what was best for them, and they did what was best for their child. They didn't stay together until I was 18 years old just "for me," as that seems to be what a lot of parents do. If that would have been the case, I can almost guarantee our situation would be very different.

Whether I liked the idea or not, I made the attempt to understand that my parents might actually be better off if they weren't married, even if that same, reoccurring thought was there: the hope that my parents would get back together. I put that happy thought in the back of mind because I wanted it to always remain there. That idea of my parents getting back together gave me a warm, cozy feeling that I didn't want to get rid of. I really did think that possibility was completely lost forever, but soon enough, that thought might not have seemed so far-fetched anymore.

Even before we had left for the Las Vegas trip, my father and his brother knew that the house had to be sold. The house that my dad and his family had lived in for 42 years, and my father and I ten years. So, after coming back from from the trip with my parents, it was time to let, yet another house that contained so many memories from multiple generations, including the better part of my father's childhood, as well as my own, go. The house itself was over one hundred years old, but man, was it absolutely gorgeous. It took some time, but after about five or six months, the process of finding a new owner was over. The beautiful, big, white, asymmetrical house surrounded by green flora was sold. Just like that, gone to a family of five, who would make their own memories in that place. It felt like the house was being passed down to a new generation, even if we didn't know the people. So after everything that had to do with the house had ended, what was my father's plan? Would he stay in the same town? What would he do? Valentina, although her and my father were happily still together, had moved to Ohio a few months after my Grandma passed away. My dad did not want to move to another state. So, there was only one path that he could have taken that wouldn't have been possible if my parents' situation was any lesser than it was: to move in with my mom. And he did.

Visualize yourself as an outsider, and hearing of my parents being apart for more than ten years now, move back in together. It was hard to believe at first for me too. I understand something of the like happening if the two were getting back together, that just makes sense, but this was different. Two people that were, at one time, at what felt like a point of no return, never to think of living with one another ever again, back where they were once before. A situation like that is unheard of to me. Now, I want you to hypothetically (or not) use your mind's eye to see your parents who have been divorced for a decade or longer, living under the same roof once again. Or sharing the same house with your ex-husband, who you've merely seen when you see your kids again. If you've been subject to an older divorce, that thought probably hasn't even crossed your mind in years. Then, imagine what the rest of the family must think about them living together again. The questions would absolutely fly all over the place. Were they getting back together? Is this really happening? What is going on? Was it finally time that they worked everything out? No, it wasn't that. My parents had simply become such good friends, better than what they were when they were part of the 'old ball and chain,' so much so that they were so comfortable and trusting of each other. They moved back in with each other, with me at the epicenter, finally having one house between the three of us. And I must say, it felt surreal – no – beyond surreal. I hadn't realized how much I truly missed the feeling of us three living in the same house again.

If you're a child of divorce, you know how hectic it can be going to and from houses, and then think about that feeling of not having to go to each house every week, or every few days, or even every other month. The fact is, the sentiment of being under the same roof again is unmatched. Not having to worry about taking your possessions from house to house, having all of your clothes in one place, and just waking up to two parents in the same house, after being split for so long might just be one of the best feelings in the world. Age doesn't matter when most of your life, your parents have been apart.

We ended up right back where we started. Sure, my parents weren't back together, but it was the next best thing. Just seeing my parents together, living in the same house, was good enough for me.

One could say it's almost the end of a fairy tale, but this can't be a fairy tale, because it's a true story. It's my family's true story.

My father lived in same house as my mother for two whole months, until he found a new place to make his own. Believe it or not, the house he found was in the same neighborhood where I spent my years as a newborn and toddler. The same neighborhood where my mother, father, and I began as a family. It was great for him, if anything a little big, but he was living where he wanted, the neighborhood and town where memories did reside. In the end, that time that us three lived together again couldn't have been better, and just writing this is giving me butterflies, wanting that feeling of the trio residing under the same roof. Nevertheless, during those two months, it felt more like two best friends living together as roommates more than anything, except those two roommates just happen to have a son living with them as well. One extremely happy son.

No matter one's situation with divorce, happiness is possible. Never give up on your family, and that doesn't mean have hopeful wishes towards parents getting back together, or even in my situation, your parents moving back in together. Just know that you were once a trio, quad, whatever, before the split, and that there was once love between you all, and that that love should never leave one's heart, or head. That feeling of being a family will be there. No matter how bad things got at one point, a broken family can always be redeemed. Divorce is many things, but in the end, no matter what you call it, it's about what is best for the whole family. It's about *the* family. For my trio, it was just meant to be the way that it was, and at this point, I wouldn't want it any other way.

To this day, my parents remain as close as they ever were, as best friends. My mother and father talk every few days, if not weekly, even randomly sending each other motivational paragraph-sized texts, just to spice up the other/s day.

My father comes over almost every major holiday, including Christmas eve, and has dinner with not only my mother and I, but our entire family.

I still see hints of the love that once was between my parents. Whether it be my mother calling and saying I love you guys at the end of the call, or my father talking about how much of an absolute inspiration my mother is.

Even though they are no longer married, I do believe the love between them never went anywhere, at least I don't think it did. Maybe the attraction, but not the love. And me? Together or not, I'm just happy I get to call them my parents.

Divorce II

Many friends and people that I know have gone through a divorce, most being the children of the two that ended it. If you haven't gone through it yourself, there's no doubt you know at least one parent or child that has gone through a divorce as well. I'm not going to mention anyone specific here, but I grew up around divorce, seeing it everywhere around me, and it is certainly different for everyone. Divorce isn't just some thing that is exactly the same every time. Think of divorce more as the entire spectrum of colors, with each color having a different hue, and each hue having a different tone. Basically, sure, some colors might look similar, but they're not. They're different. I would say our color is specific to my family, as is everyone else's that went through something like I did. I'm extremely lucky to have gone through what I did, the way I did, but who is to say you aren't lucky as well? Obviously my family didn't just patch itself up. All three of us worked at making our relationship together as a family as smooth as possible, for each other's sake.

There is one thing I would like to note, though, about my parents' divorce that I believe had a significant part in being the glue that kept most of the pieces together. It might be clear to some, but I feel that it is extremely crucial to the relationship between not only you and your parents, but to the relationship between mother and father as well, to stay close with them. Check up on each other once in a while. See how they're doing. In this case, if you're the parents, ensure that you're children are doing okay. Drop your dukes for a little, at least. Talk to them about what is, or was, going on between husband and wife. For me, I believe that if the three of us didn't put in the effort to stay close each other, or at least check up on each other, things would not have been the same. Everyone has a role to play in a divorce, even staying out of heated affairs, and not taking sides is part of it as the children. Now, I'm not saying to justify violent fights, to right wrongs that are un-rightable, or to sit in on a conversation you probably shouldn't hear, but you are a family after all. It's important to, at the very least, *understand* each other, and the perspective each member is coming from, no matter the circumstance. But parents, NEVER put any pressure on the children to fix something that was broken between you and your spouse. That isn't their job, it's your job. If the children want to help, great. If not, don't force them into it. Doing something like that is like doing damage to something that doesn't need done. And that isn't fair to the kids. Your kid's aren't your bargaining chip for something you want out of divorce, whether that's material items, or you're trying to "win over" your children's love from your once significant other. Don't use your kids. Act like adults.

I have seen various kinds of divorce throughout my life, save a few particular cases I'm sure, and I have noticed that there are definitely common themes throughout each one. From the father abandoning his family when the kids were merely a few years old, to a mother leaving when the father was catastrophically ill, because she merely wasn't happy. Even with the different "colors" of divorce, there appears to always be one obvious, guaranteed theme to run through each case, and that is blame. Whether it be one parent or both, someone is held responsible for the split. Maybe the relationship was forced to the edge of divorce because one of the parents didn't try to fix what was going on. For my parents, both realized that it was equally both of their fault, eventually. Either way, with a divorce, a mess was made, no matter who caused it. But messes can be cleaned up, although it will just sit there if nothing is actually done about it. What I'm saying is, yes, blame is part of that reality, but it's pointless and counter-productive to dwell on it. Sure, you might want to make it known that Joe spilled the drink on the table and not you, but tell him how to clean it up, or better yet, *help* him clean it up, because you know it will go faster. See what I'm getting at here? Listen, the point is, is that divorce is always a two-way street, both the cause of it, and the aftermath. Unless someone does something absolutely unforgivable, problems can be solved. You just have to put in effort. A broken window won't fix itself.

I get that by the way I might have put things, it may appear that one just needs to go through the divorce and act like nothing is happening, or happened, at all. That is absolutely false. Acting stoic doesn't help anyone, and neither does keeping your thoughts to yourself. I truly believe nostalgia is the strongest human emotion, and when it comes into play, it comes in like a wrecking ball. Rose-colored glasses are a real thing. Nostalgia can be blinding. It's okay to reminisce about the good old days, specifically, maybe when you and your ex-spouse, or parents, were together, or a time when the three (or more) of you were all having an amazing time together. In fact, it's vital to remember the good times you've had with your family, and the things you associate with them, rather than mull over the bad times. I believe the past is important, whether it's full of good or bad, it's there, own it; use it; be proud of who you are and your family is. Don't sit there and tell others, "I 'survived' my divorce," because unless one partner is being a merciless piece of trash, or holding one child as a psychological hostage, or demanding more and more unnecessary things in order to "win" the divorce, it shouldn't be war. Divorce should be treated more like a diplomatic meeting instead, except not over the rights for something, but for compromise. Even with that being said, it seems that more and more divorces are being treated like wars, sadly. No matter how many years go by, divorce is still divorce.

Maybe it has been going on for a long time, but there seems to be this growing trend of the father always being the bad guy in a divorce/relationship, no matter what he did or didn't do. Now, I'm not trying to say that fathers get a free pass, or anything like that, not at all. It just appears that men are being automatically labeled as not deserving to see their child after a divorce, because...why? I'm not trying to stir anything up, but I had to bring up this apparently asinine thought. I believe that children need both parents in their life. Obviously, there are cases where the father/mother shouldn't see their children for a mere second, or a mother or father are unlucky enough to raise their children alone, but in a relationship that isn't violent, hostile, or anything like that, shouldn't the child deserve to see both parents if they want to be in each other's lives? Having two parents is extremely important in a child's life. Honestly, if my parent's divorce ended any other way, I'm not sure how my life would have turned out. If either parent would have stopped me from seeing the other parent, I would have fought it. My life wouldn't be the same without having both my mom and dad in it, and I'm positive other kids of divorce would agree (I don't think my parents lives would have been remotely the same either, and I think both of them would rightfully agree with me). There of course will be other cases where that may not be possible, but if it is, why not help your children out, be civil, and let them see their mom/dad? There are no sides to this, a mother and father need to see their children, and mainly, children need to see both of their parents.

An Ending

There are examples of every kind of divorce out there, and despite what I said at the beginning, there very well could be one just like mine (or yours). The important part is this, always remember, you aren't alone in what you're going or have gone through, as someone else has most likely gone through it as well. I felt that my particular story needed to be told and heard, because it shows that divorce doesn't have to be ruthless; divorce doesn't have to be a war; divorce doesn't have to be bad. This whole divorce thing is suppose to be a team effort. I really want to terminate –no – obliterate this way of thinking that divorce automatically means a civil war between a family. When my grandma would ask me, "are you okay? It's terrible what your father did to your mother. I just can't imagine what you're going through," I understood why she was asking, but that proves my point. In the past, people thought divorce meant dark times, but it doesn't have to be that way. Divorce is about making peace with someone you love, or used to love. Divorce is not only deciding about what is best for you, but you're entire family. It's about what's best for the kids.

By the way, my grandma hasn't asked that question in almost ten years. Wounds heal, and people move on.

Before I finish my brief story, I do want to say that, even though we are all happy where we're at, if my parents had to undo the mistakes they made, I think they would. Not that I think they wouldn't get divorced, but I think reflecting back, maybe it wouldn't have happened, or so I like to imagine.

As I said before, this wasn't meant to be a lesson in divorce, what to expect from it, or some form of psychoanalysis on the effects of it. It also wasn't suppose to be about me, but to be a look into my family's experience with divorce, and how I remember it. I wanted to share it because I thought it was special. We've been through more than plenty together, and I'm proud of that. I wanted everyone to have a peek into what it's like being the child of an exceptional divorce.

About the Story and Author

A Brief Story of an Exceptional Divorce truly started to form when Alec came to the full realization that he didn't have the most uniform life when it came to his family, and the events that occurred regarding them. Because of that, Alec wanted this tale to include a little bit of everything: the events, people, and feelings surrounding the divorce, not just abundant information on a single thing.

You know that Alec Thein is a child of divorce, what you might not know is that it was never his intention to become a writer, let alone write anything he wasn't required to after graduating from high school. It wasn't until after attaining his degree in Game Design, that Alec realized he had enjoyed his writing classes far more than what he was in there to do, design video games.

When Alec isn't writing, he's probably attempting to produce some obscure piece of music for a short film, or watching an extremely slow paced horror flick.

A very special thanks to you, the reader.

Look out for more Brief Stories by Alec Thein!

Made in the USA
Middletown, DE
15 March 2020